Boug

Bookrong.

on 25ᵏ: October 1989.

David in charge.

THE CALENDAR
OF THE
SOUL

by
Rudolf Steiner

The Anthroposophic Press
Hudson, New York

This translation of
Anthroposophischer Seelenkalender
(included in Vol. 40 of the Bibliographical Survey
1961) was made by Ruth and Hans Pusch

Second, revised Edition 1988

Library of Congress Cataloging-in-Publication Data

Steiner, Rudolf, 1861-1925.
  The calendar of the soul.

  English and German.
  "This translation of Anthroposophischer Seelenka-
lender (included in Vol. 40 of the Bibliographical
Survey 1961) was made by Ruth and Hans Pusch"—
T.p. verso.
  I. Title.
PT2639.T4A8413   1988   831'.912   88-10523

ISBN 0-88010-263-2

PREFACE TO THE
SECOND EDITION (1918)

The course of the year has its own life. With this life the human soul can unfold a feeling-unison. If the soul opens itself to the influences that speak so variously to it week by week, it will find the right perception of itself. Thereby the soul will feel forces growing within that will strengthen it. It will observe that such inward forces want to be awakened—awakened by the soul's ability to partake in the meaningful course of the world as it comes to life in the rhythms of time. Thereby the soul becomes fully aware of the delicate, yet vital threads that exist between itself and the world into which it has been born.

In this calendar a verse is inscribed for each week. This will enable the soul to participate actively in the progressing life of the year as it unfolds from week to week. Each verse should resound in the soul as it unites with the life of the year. A healthy feeling of "at one-ness" with the course of Nature, and from this a vigorous "finding of oneself" is here intended, in the belief that, for the soul, a feeling-unison with the world's course as unfolded in these verses is something for which the soul longs when it rightly understands itself.

—Rudolf Steiner

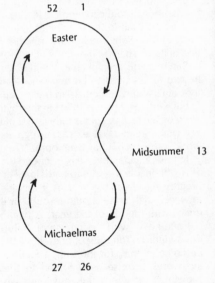

52   1

Easter

40   Midwinter

Midsummer   13

Michaelmas

27   26

CORRESPONDING VERSES OF THE
CALENDAR OF THE SOUL

It is apparent that the Calendar of the Soul is composed of corresponding verses which divide the year into two halves, from Easter to Michaelmas, and back again to Easter. For the translator, the most important task is to bring the corresponding verses into harmony with each other. By printing them side by side, each verse can be experienced with its 'octave' of the corresponding one.

But something else comes to expression in letting them speak side by side. Their relationship follows a certain law of evolution. Out of the whole evolve the parts, and this is the meaning of subtraction. We number the verses from 1 to 52 according to the weeks of the year, Easter to Easter. And now a double subtraction has to take place. We have one verse, say Number 5 for the fifth week; to find its correspondence, we must subtract 1 from our 5, which leads to 4 . . . and then subtract the 4 from 52, resulting in 48, the verse we are looking for. It is necesssary each time to subtract from the verse number and then from the whole.

This tracing of the related weeks is a gesture akin to the process of evolution. Out of the majestic unfolding of macrocosmic forces, the microcosmic worlds came into being. We ourselves followed this same process of subtraction by evolving by degrees the consciousness of self. It was a process of diminution by which we slowly exchanged our ancient clairvoyant vision, embracing totality, for our present earth-bound sight and mind, geographically conditioned by the existence in a physical body.

Subtracting means, therefore, on the one hand a diminishing, but on the other it creates a new principle of evolution, that of polarity. Not only are the parts a contrast to the whole, but also the parts themselves form opposites. There is no better description of the process than the one Emerson gave in his essay "Compensation:"

"Polarity, or action and reaction, we meet in every part of nature; in darkness and light; in heat and cold; in the ebb and flow of waters; in male and female; in the inspiration and expiration of plants and animals; in the systole and diastole of the heart; in the centrifugal and centripetal gravity . . . If the south attracts, the north repels. To empty here, you must condense there. The value of the universe contrives to throw itself into every point. If the good is there, so is the evil; if the affinity, so the repulsion; if the force, so the limitation . . . Thus is the universe alive. All things are moral. That soul which within us is a sentiment, outside of us is a law."

What lived in Emerson's mind underlies the style and composition of these weekly verses. And it is the human being who must reach a stage of compensation, of balance between the opposites, enhancing the polarities to forces of inner growth and maturity. It is a most invigorating development when it is practiced year after year in faithful succession. By combining the two corresponding verses in the mind, we gain a new insight into the workings of that which is outside and that which lives within.

—Hans Pusch

A NOTE ON THE DATES IN THE CALENDAR

The dates above the verses relate to the manuscript of the first edition, which covered the year 1912/13. When he was questioned about the change of dates that occurs from year to year, Rudolf Steiner stressed that one must always begin with the first verse at Easter. Thus, the change in dates is not important because three successive verses of the Calendar are always kept in the same mood.

THE CALENDAR
OF THE
SOUL

When from the depths of soul
The spirit turns to the life of worlds
And beauty wells from wide expanses,
Then out of heaven's distances
Streams life-strength into human bodies,
Uniting by its mighty energy
The spirit's being with our human life.

Wenn aus den Seelentiefen
Der Geist sich wendet zu dem Weltensein
Und Schönheit quillt aus Raumesweiten,
Dann zieht aus Himmelsfernen
Des Lebens Kraft in Menschenleiber
Und einet, machtvoll wirkend,
Des Geistes Wesen mit dem Menschensein.

SPRING

When out of world-wide spaces
The sun speaks to the human mind,
And gladness from the depths of soul
Becomes, in seeing, one with light,
Then rising from the sheath of self,
Thoughts soar to distances of space
And dimly bind
The human being to the spirit's life.

Wenn aus den Weltenweiten
Die Sonne spricht zum Menschensinn
Und Freude aus den Seelentiefen
Dem Licht sich eint im Schauen,
Dann ziehen aus der Selbstheit Hülle
Gedanken in die Raumesfernen
Und binden dumpf
Des Menschen Wesen an des Geistes Sein.

Into our inner being
The riches of the senses pour.
The Cosmic Spirit finds itself
Reflected in the human eye,
Which ever must renew its strength
From out that spirit source.

Ins Innre des Menschenwesens
Ergiesst der Sinne Reichtum sich,
Es findet sich der Weltengeist
Im Spiegelbild des Menschenauges,
Das seine Kraft aus ihm
Sich neu erschaffen muss.

Out in the sense-world's glory
The power of thought gives up
   its separate being,
And spirit worlds discover
Again their human offspring,
Who germinates in them
But in itself must find
The fruit of soul.

Ins Äussre des Sinnesalls
Verliert Gedankenmacht ihr Eigensein;
Es finden Geisteswelten
Den Menschensprossen wieder,
Der seinen Keim in ihnen,
Doch seine Seelenfrucht
In sich muss finden.

Thus to the human ego speaks
In mighty revelation,
Unfolding its inherent powers,
The joy of growth throughout the world:
I carry into you my life
From its enchanted bondage
And so attain my truest goal.

Es spricht zum Menschen-Ich,
Sich machtvoll offenbarend
Und seines Wesens Kräfte lösend,
Des Weltendaseins Werdelust:
In dich mein Leben tragend
Aus seinem Zauberbanne,
Erreiche ich mein wahres Ziel.

Thus to the World-All speaks,
In self-forgetfulness
And mindful of its primal state,
The growing human I:
In you, if I can free myself
From fetters of my selfhood,
I fathom my essential being.

Es spricht zum Weltenall,
Sich selbst vergessend
Und seines Urstands eingedenk,
Des Menschen wachsend Ich:
In dir, befreiend mich
Aus meiner Eigenheiten Fessel,
Ergründe ich mein echtes Wesen.

I feel the force of cosmic life:
Thus speaks my clarity of thought,
Recalling its own spirit growth
Through nights of cosmic darkness,
And to the new approach of cosmic day
It turns its inward rays of hope.

Ich fühle Kraft des Weltenseins:
So spricht Gedankenklarheit,
Gedenkend eignen Geistes Wachsen
In finstern Weltennächten,
Und neigt dem nahen Weltentage
Des Innern Hoffnungsstrahlen.

I sense a kindred nature to my own:
Thus speaks perceptive feeling
As in the sun-illumined world
It merges with the floods of light;
To thinking's clarity
My feeling would give warmth
And firmly bind as one
The human being and the world.

Ich fühle Wesen meines Wesens:
So spricht Empfindung,
Die in der sonnerhellten Welt
Mit Lichtesfluten sich vereint;
Sie will dem Denken
Zur Klarheit Wärme schenken
Und Mensch und Welt
In Einheit fest verbinden.

Within the light that out of world-wide heights
Would stream with power toward the soul,
May certainty of cosmic thinking
Arise to solve the soul's enigmas—
And focusing its mighty rays,
Awaken love in human hearts.

Im Lichte, das aus Weltenhöhen
Der Seele machtvoll fliessen will,
Erscheine, lösend Seelenrätsel,
Des Weltendenkens Sicherheit,
Versammelnd seiner Strahlen Macht,
Im Menschenherzen Liebe weckend.

Within the light that out of spirit depths
Weaves germinating power into space
And manifests the gods' creative work:
Within its shine, the soul's true being
Is widened into worldwide life
And resurrected
From narrow selfhood's inner power.

Im Lichte, das aus Geistestiefen
Im Raume fruchtbar webend
Der Götter Schaffen offenbart:
In ihm erscheint der Seele Wesen
Geweitet zu dem Weltensein
Und auferstanden
Aus enger Selbstheit Innenmacht.

There will arise out of the world's great womb,
Quickening the senses' life, the joy of growth.
Now may it find my strength of thought
Well armed by powers divine
Which strongly live within my being.

Es will erstehen aus dem Weltenschosse,
Den Sinnenschein erquickend, Werdelust.
Sie finde meines Denkens Kraft
Gerüstet durch die Gotteskräfte,
Die kräftig mir im Innern leben.

There has arisen from its narrow limits
My self and finds itself
As revelation of all worlds
Within the sway of time and space;
The world, as archetype divine,
Displays to me at every turn
The truth of my own likeness.

Es ist erstanden aus der Eigenheit
Mein Selbst und findet sich
Als Weltenoffenbarung
In Zeit- und Raumeskräften;
Die Welt, sie zeigt mir überall
Als göttlich Urbild
Des eignen Abbilds Wahrheit.

The world is threatening to stun
The inborn forces of my soul;
Now, memory, come forth
From spirit depths, enkindling light;
Invigorate my inward sight
Which only by the strength of will
Is able to sustain itself.

Die Welt, sie drohet zu betäuben
Der Seele eingeborene Kraft;
Nun trete du, Erinnerung,
Aus Geistestiefen leuchtend auf
Und stärke mir das Schauen,
Das nur durch Willenskräfte
Sich selbst erhalten kann.

My self is threatening to fly forth,
Lured strongly by the world's enticing light.
Come forth, prophetic feeling,
Take up with strength your rightful task:
Replace in me the power of thought
Which in the senses' glory
Would gladly lose itself.

Mein Selbst, es drohet zu entfliehen,
Vom Weltenlichte mächtig angezogen.
Nun trete du mein Ahnen
In deine Rechte kräftig ein,
Ersetze mir des Denkens Macht,
Das in der Sinne Schein
Sich selbst verlieren will.

My power of thought grows firm
United with the spirit's birth.
It lifts the senses' dull attractions
To bright-lit clarity.
When soul-abundance
Desires union with the world's becoming,
Must senses' revelation
Receive the light of thinking.

Es festigt sich Gedankenmacht
Im Bunde mit der Geistgeburt,
Sie hellt der Sinne dumpfe Reize
Zur vollen Klarheit auf.
Wenn Seelenfülle
Sich mit dem Weltenwerden einen will,
Muss Sinnesoffenbarung
Des Denkens Licht empfangen.

The senses' might grows strong
United with the gods' creative work;
It presses down my power of thinking
Into a dreamlike dullness.
When godly being
Desires union with my soul,
Must human thinking
In quiet dream-life rest content.

Es wächst der Sinne Macht
Im Bunde mit der Götter Schaffen,
Sie drückt des Denkens Kraft
Zur Traumes Dumpfheit mir herab.
Wenn göttlich Wesen
Sich meiner Seele einen will,
Muss menschlich Denken
Im Traumessein sich still bescheiden.

In reaching for new sense attractions,
Soul-clarity would fill,
Mindful of spirit-birth attained,
The world's bewildering, sprouting growth
With the creative will of my own thinking.

Ergreifend neue Sinnesreize
Erfüllet Seelenklarheit,
Eingedenk vollzogener Geistgeburt,
Verwirrend sprossend Weltenwerden
Mit meines Denkens Schöpferwillen.

When I forget the narrow will of self,
The cosmic warmth that heralds summer's glory
Fills all my soul and spirit;
To lose myself in light
Is the command of spirit vision
And intuition tells me strongly:
O lose yourself to find yourself.

Vergessend meine Willenseigenheit
Erfüllet Weltenwärme sommerkündend
Mir Geist und Seelenwesen;
Im Licht mich zu verlieren
Gebietet mir das Geistesschauen,
Und kraftvoll kündet Ahnung mir:
Verliere dich, um dich zu finden.

43. Forty-third Week (January 26-February 1)

In winter's depths is kindled
True spirit life with glowing warmth;
It gives to world appearance,
Through forces of the heart, the power to be.
Grown strong, the human soul defies
With inner fire the coldness of the world.

In winterlichen Tiefen
Erwarmt des Geistes wahres Sein;
Es gibt dem Weltenscheine
Durch Herzenskräfte Daseinsmächte;
Der Weltenkälte trotzt erstarkend
Das Seelenfeuer im Menscheninnern.

To summer's radiant heights
The sun in shining majesty ascends;
It takes my human feeling
Into its own wide realms of space.
Within my inner being stirs
Presentiment which heralds dimly,
You shall in future know:
A godly being now has touched you.

Zu sommerlichen Höhen
Erhebt der Sonne leuchtend Wesen sich;
Es nimmt mein menschlich Fühlen
In seine Raumesweiten mit.
Erahnend regt im Innern sich
Empfindung, dumpf mir kündend,
Erkennen wirst du einst:
Dich fühlte jetzt ein Gotteswesen.

In this the shrouding gloom of winter
The soul feels ardently impelled
To manifest its innate strength,
To guide itself to realms of darkness,
Anticipating thus
Through warmth of heart the sense-world's
    revelation.

Es ist in diesem Winterdunkel
Die Offenbarung eigner Kraft
Der Seele starker Trieb,
In Finsternisse sie zu lenken
Und ahnend vorzufühlen
Durch Herzenswärme Sinnesoffenbarung.

In this the sun's high hour it rests
With you to understand these words of wisdom:
Surrendered to the beauty of the world,
Be stirred with new-enlivened feeling;
The human I can lose itself
And find itself within the cosmic I.

Es ist in dieser Sonnenstunde
An dir, die weise Kunde zu erkennen:
An Weltenschönheit hingegeben
In dir dich fühlend zu durchleben:
Verlieren kann das Menschen-Ich
Und finden sich im Welten-Ich.

The soul's creative might
Strives outward from the heart's own core
To kindle and inflame god-given powers
In human life to right activity;
The soul thus shapes itself
In human loving and in human working.

Der Seele Schaffensmacht,
Sie strebet aus dem Herzensgrunde,
Im Menschenleben Götterkräfte
Zu rechtem Wirken zu entflammen,
Sich selber zu gestalten
In Menschenliebe und im Menschenwerke.

12. St. John's Tide (June 24)

The radiant beauty of the world
Compels my inmost soul to free
God-given powers of my nature
That they may soar into the cosmos,
To take wing from myself
And trustingly to seek myself
In cosmic light and cosmic warmth.

Der Welten Schönheitsglanz,
Er zwinget mich aus Seelentiefen
Des Eigenlebens Götterkräfte
Zum Weltenfluge zu entbinden;
Mich selber zu verlassen,
Vertrauend nur mich suchend
In Weltenlicht und Weltenwärme.

And when I live in spirit depths
And dwell within my soul's foundations,
There streams from love-worlds of the heart,
To fill the vain delusion of the self,
The fiery power of the cosmic Word.

Und bin ich in den Geistestiefen,
Erfüllt in meinen Seelengründen
Aus Herzens Liebewelten
Der Eigenheiten leerer Wahn
Sich mit des Weltenwortes Feuerkraft.

And when I live in senses' heights,
There flames up deep within my soul
Out of the spirit's fiery worlds
The gods' own word of truth:
In spirit sources seek expectantly
To find your spirit kinship.

Und bin ich den Sinneshöhen,
So flammt in meinen Seelentiefen
Aus Geistes Feuerwelten
Der Götter Wahrheitswort:
In Geistesgründen suche ahnend
Dich geistverwandt zu finden.

Surrendering to spirit revelation
I gain the light of cosmic being;
The power of thinking, growing clearer,
Gains strength to give myself to me,
And quickening there frees itself
From thinker's energy my sense of self.

An Geistesoffenbarung hingegeben
Gewinne ich des Weltenwesens Licht,
Gedankenkraft, sie wächst
Sich klärend mir mich selbst zu geben,
Und weckend löst sich mir
Aus Denkermacht das Selbstgefühl.

SUMMER

Surrendering to senses' revelation
I lost the drive of my own being,
And dreamlike thinking seemed
To daze and rob me of my self.
Yet quickening there draws near
In sense appearance cosmic thinking.

An Sinnesoffenbarung hingegeben
Verlor ich Eigenwesens Trieb,
Gedankentraum, er schien
Betäubend mir das Selbst zu rauben,
Doch weckend nahet schon
Im Sinnenschein mir Weltendenken.

38. Christmas

The spirit child within my soul
I feel freed of enchantment.
In heart-high gladness has
The holy cosmic Word engendered
The heavenly fruit of hope,
Which grows rejoicing into worlds afar
Out of my being's godly roots.

Ich fühle wie entzaubert
Das Geisteskind im Seelenschoss;
Es hat in Herzenshelligkeit
Gezeugt das heilige Weltenwort
Der Hoffnung Himmelsfrucht,
Die jubelnd wächst in Weltenfernen
Aus meines Wesens Gottesgrund.

I feel enchanted weaving
Of spirit within outer glory.
In dullness of the senses
It has enwrapt my being
In order to bestow the strength
Which in its narrow bounds my I
Is powerless to give itself.

Ich fühle wie verzaubert
Im Weltenschein des Geistes Weben:
Es hat in Sinnesdumpfheit
Gehüllt mein Eigenwesen,
Zu schenken mir die Kraft:
Die, ohnmächtig sich selbst zu geben,
Mein Ich in seinen Schranken ist.

WINTER

To carry spirit light into world-winter-night
My heart is ardently impelled,
That shining seeds of soul
Take root in grounds of worlds
And Word Divine through senses' darkness
Resounds, transfiguring all life.

Zu tragen Geisteslicht in Weltenwinternacht
Erstrebet selig meines Herzens Trieb,
Dass leuchtend Seelenkeime
In Weltengründen wurzeln,
Und Gotteswort im Sinnesdunkel
Verklärend alles Sein durchtönt.

To bear in inward keeping spirit bounty
Is stern command of my prophetic feeling,
That ripened gifts divine
Maturing in the depths of soul
To selfhood bring their fruits.

Zu bergen Geistgeschenk im Innern,
Gebietet strenge mir mein Ahnen,
Dass reifend Gottesgaben
In Seelengründen fruchtend
Der Selbstheit Früchte bringen.

Within my being's depths there speaks,
Intent on revelation,
The cosmic Word mysteriously:
Imbue your labor's aims
With my bright spirit light
To sacrifice yourself through me.

In meines Wesens Tiefen spricht
Zur Offenbarung drängend
Geheimnisvoll das Weltenwort:
Erfülle deiner Arbeit Ziele
Mit meinem Geisteslichte,
Zu opfern dich durch mich.

Thus speaks the cosmic Word
That I by grace through senses' portals
Have led into my inmost soul:
Imbue your spirit depths
With my wide world horizons
To find in future time myself in you.

Es spricht das Weltenwort,
Das ich durch Sinnestore
In Seelengründe durfte führen:
Erfülle deine Geistestiefen
Mit meinen Weltenweiten,
Zu finden einstens mich in dir.

Can I know life's reality
So that it's found again
Within my soul's creative urge?
I feel that I am granted power
To make my self, as humble part,
At home within the cosmic self.

Kann ich das Sein erkennen,
Dass es sich wiederfindet
Im Seelenschaffensdrange?
Ich fühle, dass mir Macht verlieh'n,
Das eigne Selbst dem Weltenselbst
Als Glied bescheiden einzuleben.

18. Eighteenth Week (August 4-10)

Can I expand my soul
That it unites itself
With cosmic Word received as seed?
I sense that I must find the strength
To fashion worthily my soul
As fitting raiment for the spirit.

Kann ich die Seele weiten,
Dass sie sich selbst verbindet
Empfangnem Welten-Keimesworte?
Ich ahne, dass ich Kraft muss finden,
Die Seele würdig zu gestalten,
Zum Geistes-Kleide sich zu bilden.

In secret inwardly to feel
How all that I've preserved of old
Is quickened by new-risen sense of self:
This shall, awakening, pour forth cosmic forces
Into the outer actions of my life
And growing, mould me into true existence.

Geheimnisvoll das Alt-Bewahrte
Mit neuerstandnem Eigensein
Im Innern sich belebend fühlen:
Es soll erweckend Weltenkräfte
In meines Lebens Aussenwerk ergiessen
Und werdend mich ins Dasein prägen.

In secret to encompass now
With memory what I've newly got
Shall be my striving's further aim:
Thus, ever strengthening, selfhood's forces
Shall be awakened from within
And growing, give me to myself.

Geheimnisvoll das Neu-Empfang'ne
Mit der Erinnrung zu umschliessen,
Sei meines Strebens weitrer Sinn:
Er soll erstarkend Eigenkräfte
In meinem Innern wecken
Und werdend mich mir selber geben.

I feel at last the world's reality
Which, lacking the communion of my soul,
Would in itself be frosty, empty life,
And showing itself powerless
To recreate itself in souls,
Would in itself find only death.

So fühl ich erst die Welt,
Die ausser meiner Seele Miterleben
An sich nur frostig leeres Leben
Und ohne Macht sich offenbarend,
In Seelen sich von neuem schaffend,
In sich den Tod nur finden könnte.

I feel at last my life's reality
Which, severed from the world's existence,
Would in itself obliterate itself,
And building only on its own foundation,
Would in itself bring death upon itself.

So fühl ich erst mein Sein,
Das fern vom Welten-Dasein
In sich, sich selbst erlöschen
Und bauend nur auf eignem Grunde
In sich, sich selbst ertöten müsste.

I feel my own force, bearing fruit
And gaining strength to give me to the world.
My inmost being I feel charged with power
To turn with clearer insight
Toward the weaving of life's destiny.

Ich fühle fruchtend eigne Kraft
Sich stärkend mich der Welt verleihn;
Mein Eigenwesen fühl ich kraftend
Zur Klarheit sich zu wenden
Im Lebensschicksalsweben.

I feel strange power, bearing fruit
And gaining strength to give myself to me.
I sense the seed maturing
And expectation, light-filled, weaving
Within me on my selfhood's power.

Ich fühle fruchtend fremde Macht
Sich stärkend mir mich selbst verleihn,
Den Keim empfind ich reifend
Und Ahnung lichtvoll weben
Im Innern an der Selbstheit Macht.

The light from spirit depths
Strives to ray outwards, sun-imbued;
Transformed to forceful will of life
It shines into the senses' dullness
To bring to birth the powers
Whereby creative forces, soul-impelled,
Shall ripen into human deeds.

Das Licht aus Geistestiefen,
Nach aussen strebt es sonnenhaft:
Es wird zur Lebenswillenskraft
Und leuchtet in der Sinne Dumpfheit,
Um Kräfte zu entbinden,
Die Schaffensmächte aus Seelentrieben
Im Menschenwerke reifen lassen.

The light from world-wide spaces
Works on within with living power;
Transformed to light of soul
It shines into the spirit depths
To bring to birth the fruits
Whereby out of the self of worlds
The human self in course of time shall ripen.

Das Licht aus Weltenweiten,
Im Innern lebt es kräftig fort:
Es wird zum Seelenlichte
Und leuchtet in die Geistestiefen,
Um Früchte zu entbinden,
Die Menschenselbst aus Weltenselbst
Im Zeitenlaufe reifen lassen.

There flourish in the sunlight of my soul
The ripened fruits of thinking;
To conscious self-assurance
The flow of feeling is transformed.
I can perceive now joyfully
The autumn's spirit-waking:
The winter will arouse in me
The summer of the soul.

Es spriessen mir im Seelensonnenlicht
Des Denkens reife Früchte,
In Selbstbewusstseins Sicherheit
Verwandelt alles Fühlen sich.
Empfinden kann ich freudevoll
Des Herbstes Geisterwachen:
Der Winter wird in mir
Den Seelensommer wecken.

There dims in damp autumnal air
The senses' luring magic;
The light's revealing radiance
Is dulled by hazy veils of mist.
In distances around me I can see
The autumn's winter sleep;
The summer's life has yielded
Itself into my keeping.

Es dämpfet herbstlich sich
Der Sinne Reizesstreben;
In Lichtesoffenbarung mischen
Der Nebel dumpfe Schleier sich.
Ich selber schau in Raumesweiten
Des Herbstes Winterschlaf.
Der Sommer hat an mich
Sich selber hingegeben.

To fan the spark of thinking into flame
By my own strong endeavor,
To read life's inner meaning
Out of the cosmic spirit's fount of strength:
This is my summer heritage,
My autumn solace, and my winter hope.

Sich selbst des Denkens Leuchten
Im Innern kraftvoll zu entfachen,
Erlebtes sinnvoll deutend
Aus Weltengeistes Kräftequell,
Ist mir nun Sommererbe,
Ist Herbstesruhe und auch Winterhoffnung.

Unceasingly itself creating,
Soul life becomes aware of self;
The cosmic spirit, striving on,
Renews itself by self-cognition,
And from the darkness of the soul
Creates the fruit of self-engendered will.

Sich selbst erschaffend stets,
Wird Seelensein sich selbst gewahr;
Der Weltengeist, er strebet fort
In Selbsterkenntnis neu belebt
Und schafft aus Seelenfinsternis
Des Selbstsinns Willensfrucht.

I can, in newly quickened inner life,
Sense wide horizons in myself.
The force and radiance of my thought—
Coming from soul's sun power—
Can solve the mysteries of life,
And grant fulfillment now to wishes
Whose wings have long been lamed by hope.

Ich kann im Innern neu belebt
Erfühlen eignen Wesens Weiten
Und krafterfüllt Gedankenstrahlen
Aus Seelensonnenmacht
Den Lebensrätseln lösend spenden,
Erfüllung manchem Wunsche leihen,
Dem Hoffnung schon die Schwingen lähmte.

I can belong now to myself
And shining spread my inner light
Into the dark of space and time.
Toward sleep is urging all creation,
But inmost soul must stay awake
And carry wakefully sun's glowing
Into the winter's icy flowing.

Ich darf nun mir gehören
Und leuchtend breiten Innenlicht
In Raumes- und in Zeitenfinsternis.
Zum Schlafe drängt natürlich Wesen,
Der Seele Tiefen sollen wachen
Und wachend tragen Sonnengluten
In kalte Winterfluten.

AUTUMN

When to my being's depths I penetrate,
There stirs expectant longing
That self-observing, I may find myself
As gift of summer sun, a seed
That warming lives in autumn mood
As germinating force of soul.

In meines Wesens Tiefen dringen:
Erregt ein ahnungsvolles Sehnen,
Dass ich mich selbstbetrachtend finde,
Als Sommersonnengabe, die als Keim
In Herbstesstimmung wärmend lebt
Als meiner Seele Kräftetrieb.

26. Michaelmas

O Nature, your maternal life
I bear within the essence of my will.
And my will's fiery energy
Shall steel my spirit striving,
That sense of self springs forth from it
To hold me in myself.

Natur, dein mütterliches Sein,
Ich trage es in meinem Willenswesen;
Und meines Willens Feuermacht,
Sie stählet meines Geistes Triebe,
Dass sie gebären Selbstgefühl,
Zu tragen mich in mir.